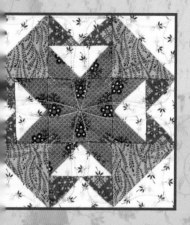

P9-CCB-132

KINDRED SPIRITS

Celebrating Pieces of the Past

By **Jill Shaulis** and **Vicki Olsen**
of **Yellow Creek Quilt Designs**

KINDRED SPIRITS

Celebrating Pieces of the Past

By **Jill Shaulis** *and* **Vicki Olsen** *of* **Yellow Creek Quilt Designs**

Editor: Kimber Mitchell
Designer: Bob Deck
Photography: Aaron T. Leimkuehler
Illustration: Eric Sears
Technical Editor: Nan Doljac
Photo Editor: Jo Ann Groves

Published by:
Kansas City Star Books
1729 Grand Blvd.
Kansas City, Missouri, USA 64108

All rights reserved
Copyright © 2013 Jill Shaulis, Vicki Olsen, and The Kansas City Star Co.

No part of this book may be reproduced, stored in a retrieval system, or transmitted in any form or by any means, electronic, mechanical, photocopying, recording or otherwise, without the prior consent of the publisher.
Exception: we grant permission to photocopy the patterns for personal use only.

No finished quilts or other projects featured in this book can be produced or sold commercially without the permission of the author and publisher.

First edition, first printing
ISBN: 9781611690941

Library of Congress Control Number: 2013939145

Printed in the United States of America by
Walsworth Publishing Co., Marceline, MO

To order copies, call StarInfo at (816) 234-4242.

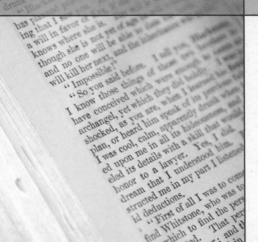

ABOUT THE AUTHORS

Vicki Olsen (left) and Jill Shaulis (right) learned to sew from their mom and participated in 4-H and Home Economics. Jill made her first quilt as a history project when she was in junior high. The two began quilting in earnest in the late 1980s and opened their shop, Sew Many Antiques, in their hometown of Pearl City, Illinois, in 1992. They now design patterns for their quilt shop, Yellow Cree Quilt Designs, which was featured in *Quilt Sampler* magazine in 2011. Jill and her husband, Dave, make their home in Lanark, Illino and have six children. Vicki and her husband, Dave, make their hor in Pearl City, Illinois, and have three children.

TABLE *of* CONTENTS

ABOUT THE PHOTOGRAPHY

Many of the photos in this book were shot in the beautifully restored John Wornall House in Kansas City's historical Brookside neighborhood. Built in 1858 by Kentucky-born John B. Wornall, this elegant Greek Revival dwelling originally sat on the Missouri frontier in the center of a 500-acre farm. It is one of four remaining Civil War period homes in the area. During the Civil War, the house was used as a field hospital for both Union and Confederate forces after the Battle of Westport.

According to tradition, the brick for the house was fired on a site 50 feet east of the house. The limestone for the home's foundation and fireplaces were quarried on Wornall's farm. The interior has been accurately restored to its period charm with authentic furnishings that illustrate why the house was once called "the most pretentious house in Kansas City."

For more information on this gracious home, visit **www.wornallhouse.org**.

INTRODUCTION

Inspired by our Grandma Stroup and our mom's never idle hands, we have both sewn since we were little and often made our own clothes. Although she did not quilt, our grandma was a wonderful seamstress and an accomplished needleworker. Our mom is also a talented seamstress and made most of our clothing when we were kids. The quilting bug hit us after Jill invited our mom to attend a beginning quilt class with her in 1989. Once Vicki saw what we were doing, she quickly jumped in. We haven't stopped quilting since!

As quilt designers, tradition has always guided our creative process. Whether we're browsing an antique quilt booth at a quilt show or exploring photos of old quilts online, we find ourselves drawn to these treasures of the past. Perhaps it's their warm colors or their connection to the busy hands of yesterday's quilters who were able to do so much with so little. Thankfully, many of these quilted treasures have endured the test of time and are still cherished today.

Despite our love of tradition, we can't resist putting our own twist on it. For example, traditional quilts such as samplers often feature only one of each block design, but we like to give them a fresh look by incorporating several of each kind into our designs. We also enjoy adapting block designs from our quilts into smaller projects such as table runners and table mats.

To help spark your creativity, we have gathered a hearty helping of traditional projects with our own unique twist. We hope you'll find the perfect project among them, or better yet, so many that you won't know where to start!

Happy Quilting!

Jill   *Vicki*

Dedication

This book is dedicated to our tireless mom, Edna Meyer, for supporting us through our many quilting endeavors. Not only did Mom and her mother, our Grandma Stroup, teach us both to sew at an early age, but she has always been willing to stand in at our quilt shop for an extra day or two on short notice when we find ourselves busy with classes or quilt shows. She's watched children, done laundry, tested patterns, and much more. Her devotion to friends and family, as well as her dedicated work ethic, are a constant source of strength and inspiration. Without her support, this book could not have been written.

ACKNOWLEDGMENTS

Our heartfelt thanks go to:

Doug Weaver for giving us this opportunity to write a book with such a wonderful company.

Kimber Mitchell—We can't imagine a better editor! You made the book production process such a pleasure!

Aaron Leimkuehler for your wonderful photographic skills and insight.

Edie McGinnis for your photo-staging skills that mesh so wonderfully with Aaron's.

Bob Deck, our designer, who brought our projects to life on the pages of this beautiful book.

Eric Sears, our illustrator, for your artistic talents in creating all the helpful diagrams that make our projects easier to follow.

Nan Doljac, our technical editor, for your keen eye in checking the accuracy of our instructions.

Marcus Brothers Textiles' Pati Violick, Windham Fabrics' Jennifer Varon, Moda Fabrics' Lissa Alexander and Debbie Outlaw, and Andover Fabrics' Gail Kessler for taking care of our fabric requests.

Dan Kolbe and Janet Graves for your wonderful quilting skills on several projects in this book—sometimes on very short notice!

Our dedicated employees, who are always there even at a moment's notice to help out in any way.

Our friends, customers, fellow quilt shop owners, and designers who have supported and encouraged our quilting habit.

Jill Shaulis

To my heart and soul, my husband, Dave. With warmth and understanding, he has supported me through euphoric highs and stressful moments. Through it all, he has never complained about fixing meals or keeping up with the laundry and household chores. He always supports me, takes pride in my passion, and has come to understand that my brain doesn't necessarily turn off even when the lights do!

I can't begin to express my thanks to my children, Todd, Scott, and Jodi. They have helped out in our quilt shop since they were small. Today, Todd and Scott tirelessly lend their guidance, creativity, and computer skills. Jodi, who is already an accomplished quilter and excellent sales person, is always helpful whether I need a sounding board or assistance at quilt shows.

To my sister, Vicki, who has always been my cheerleader, math queen, and the one who is willing to jump off just about any cliff I take her to the edge of.

Vicki Olsen

My thanks go to many but my words are few:
To my husband, Dave, who takes my long absences in stride when I retreat to the sewing room. He even takes care of the cooking. After all, a girl has to keep up her strength!

To my daughter, Sara, who picked up laundry duty in the early years and has dibs on most of my finished projects.

To my sister, Jill, who inspired me to quilt with her dream of owning a quilt shop. She had to drag me along to my first quilt class, but I eventually caught the quilting bug and have appreciated her help and encouragement along the way. If not for her, I would not have this opportunity.

And last but not least, to each and every one of you. We are blessed to have you in our lives!

TOOLS OF THE TRADE

As quilters, we all have tools we like to use that help make the quilting process go smoother. Here are some of the handy helpers we use when making our quilts.

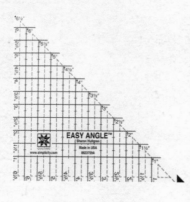

To make half-square triangle units, we like to use the **Easy Angle ruler**® because it's very accurate, and you can use the same size strip to cut your half-square triangle units as you do for other block sections. For example, for a Friendship Star, you can use the same size strip to cut the half-square triangle units as you do for the center and outer four corner squares. No funky math is needed because the ¼" is already built in! <u>The instructions in this book do NOT require this tool but here are a couple general guidelines on how to convert them for the Easy Angle if desired.</u> For detailed instructions, refer to those that come with the ruler.

1. If your block looks like the one to the right, find the measurement used to cut the center red square. That will be the size of the brown fabric and background fabric strip that you will use to create the half-square triangle units in the outer corners.

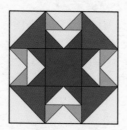

2. If your block requires Hourglass units like the one to the right, you will need to add 1" to the measurement that the center square was cut to make your strips for the half-square triangle units and Hourglass units. To quickly and easily square up units like the Hourglass, we like to use the handy **Precision Trimmer 6**®.

We often use spray starch on our blocks because it gives them a crisp look and feel, making them easier to work with. Our favorite is **Mary Ellen's Best Press**.

For projects like our *Pickle Dish* framed quilt on page 66, we love using pre-cut hexagon papers by **Paper Pieces** because they are extremely accurate and can be reused several times.

When foundation-piecing detailed patterns like our *Primitive Pineapple* framed quilt on page 73, we prefer to use a base product called **Fundation**, which holds up much better than paper when piecing such small projects.

To find these handy products, visit your local quilt shop.

ABOUT THE PROJECTS

Throughout the book, the directions allow for half-square triangles to be made larger and trimmed down for accuracy. Feel free to make the half-square triangles using any method you prefer.

Because of variances in individual sewing techniques, it is best to assemble your quilt center and measure it, then cut your borders to the exact size needed for your quilt. Border measurements listed in the cutting instructions for each project are a guideline.

Jill and Vicki cut their binding 3 inches wide and sew it to the quilt with a ⅜" seam allowance to make turning corners easier. Feel free to use whatever binding width you prefer.

BROTHERS *and* SISTERS

Finished quilt size: 72" x 91½" **Finished block size:** 18" x 18"

Designed by Jill Shaulis
Quilted by Dan Kolbe

Our family consists of three sisters and three brothers. And just like our siblings, the 12 scrappy blocks in this sampler quilt are similar yet different. They're created with six smaller block designs—made in two versions featuring two different block sizes. This creates a sense of continuity throughout the quilt, yet the blocks are scrappy in nature, giving each a unique look. An equally scrappy border adds pizzazz to the quilt, which incorporates a diverse array of my favorite fabrics—Civil War reproduction prints.

Fabric Requirements

✦ 14 fat quarters of light/cream prints for block and outer border backgrounds
✦ 6–8 fat quarters each of three different color families. Choose various values and colors within each color family, such as pinks, reds, and burgundies for the red color family. We used reds, blues and browns (including gold), and also threw in a little green for more variety.
✦ 2¼ yards brown print for sashing, inner border, and binding
✦ 5¼ yards fabric of choice for backing

> **Our project is very scrappy. If you prefer a more planned palette, use these yardage requirements:**
> ✦ 3 yards light/cream print for block and outer border backgrounds
> ✦ 1½ yards each of 3 contrasting dark/medium prints for blocks and outer border (the contrast can be in value or color)
> ✦ 2¼ yards brown print for sashing, inner border, and binding
> ✦ 5¼ yards fabric of choice for backing

Cutting Instructions

From brown print, cut:
✦ 9—2" strips the width of fabric, then sub-cut those into 8—2" x 18½" strips and 3—2" x 57½" strips for sashing
✦ 9—3" strips the width of fabric for binding

From dark/medium prints, cut:
✦ 190—2" x 5½" rectangles for pieced border
✦ 12—2" squares for border cornerstones

From light/cream print, cut:
✦ 190—2" squares for pieced border
✦ 190—2" x 2¼" rectangles for pieced border
✦ 8—2" x 4¼" rectangles for border cornerstones
✦ 4—4¼" squares for border cornerstones

Block cutting instructions are listed in the block sewing instructions on pages 12-23.

Inner border cutting instructions are listed in the **Sewing Instructions** on page 29.

Sewing Instructions
THE BLOCKS

The 12 blocks in this quilt feature six smaller block designs made in two different versions—one with four 9" blocks and one with nine 6" blocks. For each block, you will use four different prints—three medium/dark prints and one light print. For a scrappy look, use a different variety of fabrics in each block. The block cutting instructions on pages 12–22 are for ONE block only.

BLOCK 1

Cutting Instructions

From medium/dark print 1 (pink), cut:
- ✦ 1 – 3½" square for 9" blocks
- ✦ 1 – 2½" square for 6" blocks

From medium/dark print 2 (red), cut:
- ✦ 8 – 2" squares for 9" blocks
- ✦ 8 – 1½" squares for 6" blocks

From medium/dark print 3 (blue), cut:
- ✦ 1 – 2" x 17" strip for 9" blocks
- ✦ 1 – 1½" x 13" strip for 6" blocks

From light print, cut:
- ✦ 4 – 3½" squares for 9" blocks
- ✦ 1 – 2" x 17" strip for 9" blocks
- ✦ 4 – 2½" squares for 6" blocks
- ✦ 1 – 1½" x 13" strip for 6" blocks

Sewing Instructions

1. Sew together a blue print and light print strip, then press toward the blue print. Straighten an end, then cut the strip into 8—2"-wide segments for the 9" blocks OR 8—1½"-wide segments for the 6" blocks.

2. Use the segments from the previous step to create a total of four Four-Patch units per block. Set aside.

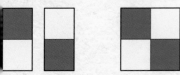

3. Mark a diagonal line from corner to corner on the wrong side of the red print square. With right sides together, layer the red print square on top of the lower left-hand corner of the larger light print square and sew on the drawn line, then press back the red triangle. You may need to stitch slightly outside of the line so that when the red triangle is pressed back, it reaches the edge of the larger light print square below it. This will give you a squared edge with which to sew this unit to the adjoining pieces later. Another option is to trim the outer section of the red print square as shown below to reveal the squared edge of the light print square underneath it, which you can use as a guide when sewing the adjoining pieces to it later. (Jill and Vicki used this technique on these types of units throughout the quilt.) Repeat this step with another red print square on the opposite side of the larger light print square as shown in the last three squares below. Then repeat to make a total of four of these units per block.

4. To complete the block, sew together four units from step 2, four units from step 3, and a 3½" pink print square for the 9" blocks OR a 2½" pink print square for the 6" blocks. Press seams toward the Four-Patch units or the center square when possible.

5. Repeat steps 1–4 to make a total of 4—9" blocks and 9—6" blocks.

BLOCK 2

Cutting Instructions

From medium/dark print 1 (black), cut:
- ✦ 1 — 3½" square for 9" blocks
- ✦ 8 — 2" squares for 9" blocks
- ✦ 1 — 2½" square for 6" blocks
- ✦ 8 — 1½" squares for 6" blocks

From medium/dark print 2 (red), cut:
- ✦ 2 — 4" squares for 9" blocks
- ✦ 2 — 3" squares for 6" blocks

From medium/dark print 3 (yellow), cut:
- ✦ 8 — 2" squares for 9" blocks
- ✦ 8 — 1½" squares for 6" blocks

From light print, cut:
- ✦ 2 — 4" squares for 9" blocks
- ✦ 8 — 2" x 3½" rectangles for 9" blocks
- ✦ 2 — 3" squares for 6" blocks
- ✦ 8 — 1½" x 2½" rectangles for 6" blocks

Sewing Instructions

1. Draw a diagonal line from corner to corner on the wrong side of 2–4" light print squares for the 9" blocks OR 2–3" light print squares for the 6" blocks. With right sides together, layer a light print square on top of a 4" red print square for the 9" blocks OR a 3" red print square for the 6" blocks. Sew ¼" from each side of the drawn line. Cut apart on the drawn line. Press seams toward the red print and trim the unit to 3½" square for the 9" blocks OR 2½" square for the 6" blocks. Repeat to make a total of four units per block. Set aside.

2. Draw a diagonal line on the wrong side of the 2" yellow print squares for the 9" blocks OR 1½" yellow print squares for the 6" blocks. With right sides together, layer a yellow print square on top of a 2" x 3½" light print rectangle for the 9" block OR 1½" x 2½" light print rectangle for the 6" block and sew on the drawn line. Trim the outer portion of the yellow print square as shown in the second unit below and press back the yellow print triangle. Repeat this with a second yellow print square on the other side of the rectangle to complete the Flying Geese unit. Repeat this step to make a total of eight Flying Geese units (four with the yellow squares and four with the black squares per block).

 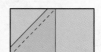 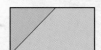

3. Sew one yellow/light print Flying Geese unit to one black/light print Flying Geese unit. Press seams toward the black/light print Flying Geese unit or press them open.

4. To complete the block, sew together the four units from step 1, the four units from step 3, and a 3½" black print square for the 9" block OR a 2½" black print square for the 6" block. Press seams toward the half-square triangle units and center square when possible.

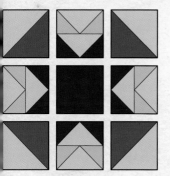

5. Repeat steps 1–4 to create a total of 4–9" blocks and 9–6" blocks.

BLOCK 3

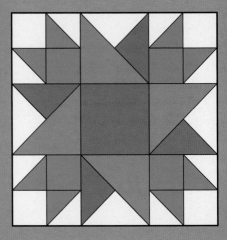

Cutting Instructions

From medium/dark print 1 (brown), cut:
- ✦ 1 – 3½" square for 9" blocks
- ✦ 2 – 4¼" squares for 9" blocks
- ✦ 1 – 2½" square for 6" blocks
- ✦ 2 – 3¼" squares for 6" blocks

From medium/dark print 2 (terra cotta), cut:
- ✦ 2 – 4" squares for 9" blocks
- ✦ 2 – 3" squares for 6" blocks

From medium/dark print 3 (blue), cut:
- ✦ 4 – 2" squares for 9" blocks
- ✦ 4 – 2½" squares for 9" blocks
- ✦ 4 – 1½" squares for 6" blocks
- ✦ 4 – 2" squares for 6" blocks

From light print, cut:
- ✦ 4 – 2" squares for 9" blocks
- ✦ 2 – 4" squares for 9" blocks
- ✦ 4 – 2½" squares for 9" blocks
- ✦ 4 – 1½" squares for 6" blocks
- ✦ 2 – 3" squares for 6" blocks
- ✦ 4 – 2" squares for 6" blocks

Sewing Instructions

1. Draw a diagonal line from corner to corner on the wrong side of the 2½" light print squares for the 9" blocks OR 2" light print squares for the 6" blocks. With right sides together, layer a light print square on top of a blue print square and sew ¼" from both sides of the drawn line. Cut apart on the drawn line. Press seams toward the blue print, and trim the units to measure 2" square for the 9" blocks OR 1½" square for the 6" blocks. Repeat to create a total of eight half-square triangle units per block.

2. Sew two of the half-square triangle units from the previous step to a blue print square and a light print square to create the following unit. Press seams toward the blue print square and light print square. Repeat to make a total of four units per block. Set aside.

3. Draw a diagonal line from corner to corner on the wrong side of the 4¼" light print squares for the 9" blocks OR 3¼" light print squares for the 6" blocks. With right sides together, layer a light print square on top of a brown print square and sew ¼" from both sides of the drawn line. Cut apart on the drawn line. Press seams toward the brown print. Repeat to create a total of four units. Cut the units in half as shown below. Toss the units specified below.

    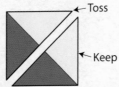

← Toss

← Keep

4. Cut the 4" terra cotta print squares for the 9" blocks OR 3" terra cotta print squares for the 6" blocks in half diagonally. Then sew a terra cotta print triangle to the brown/light print section from the previous step. The terra cotta print triangle will be slightly larger than the other section, so center the smaller one so that the edges of both triangles' long sides are even with each other as shown below. Press seams toward the terra cotta print and trim the unit to measure 3½" square for the 9" blocks OR 2½" square for the 6" blocks. Repeat to make a total of four units per block.

Wrong side of fabric

5. To complete the block, sew together the four units from step 2, the four units from step 4, and a 3½" brown print square for the 9" block OR a 2½" brown print square for the 6" block. Press seams toward the blue/light print units and center square when possible.

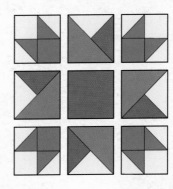

6. Repeat steps 1–5 to make a total of 4–9" blocks and 9–6" blocks.

BLOCK 4

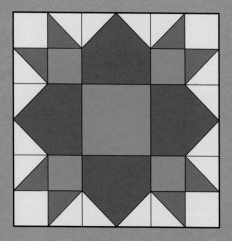

Cutting Instructions

From medium/dark print 1 (dark brown), cut:
- ✦ 4—3½" squares for 9" blocks
- ✦ 4—2½" squares for 6" blocks

From medium/dark print 2 (taupe), cut:
- ✦ 4—2" squares for 9" blocks
- ✦ 1—3½" square for 9" blocks
- ✦ 4—1½" squares for 6" blocks
- ✦ 1—2½" square for 6" blocks

From medium/dark print 3 (orange), cut:
- ✦ 4—2½" squares for 9" blocks
- ✦ 4—2" squares for 6" blocks

From light print, cut:
- ✦ 12—2" squares for 9" blocks
- ✦ 4—2½" squares for 9" blocks
- ✦ 12—1½" squares for 6" blocks
- ✦ 4—2" squares for 6" blocks

Sewing Instructions

1. Draw a diagonal line from corner to corner on the wrong side of the 8 — 2" light print squares for the 9" blocks OR 8 — 1½" light print squares for the 6" blocks. With right sides together, layer a light print square on top of the lower left-hand corner of the larger dark brown print square and sew on the drawn line. Trim the outer edge of the light print square as shown in the second square below, then press it back. Repeat this step with a second light print square in the opposite corner of the larger dark brown print square. Repeat to make a total of four units.

2. Draw a diagonal line from corner to corner on the wrong side of the 2½" light print squares for the 9" blocks OR 2" light print squares for the 6" blocks. With right sides together, layer a light print square on top of an orange print square. Sew ¼" from both sides of the drawn line and cut apart on the drawn line. Press seams toward the orange print. Repeat to create a total of eight half-square triangles per block, then trim them to measure 2" square for the 9" blocks OR 1½" square for the 6" blocks.

3. Sew two units from the previous step to a 2" light print square and a 2" taupe print square for the 9" blocks OR to a 1½" light print square and 1½" taupe print square for the 6" blocks to create the following unit. Repeat to create a total of four units per block. Press seams toward the light print square and taupe print square.

4. To complete the block, sew together the units from the previous step, the four units from step 1, and a 3½" taupe print square for the 9" blocks OR a 2½" taupe print square for the 6" blocks.

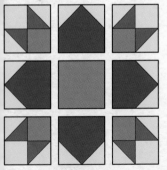

5. Repeat steps 1–4 to create a total of 4 — 9" blocks and 9 — 6" blocks.

BLOCK 5

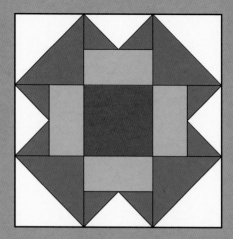

Cutting Instructions

From medium/dark print 1 (olive green), cut:
- ✦ 2—4" squares for 9" blocks
- ✦ 8—2" squares for 9" blocks
- ✦ 2—3" squares for 6" blocks
- ✦ 8—1½" squares for 6" blocks

From medium/dark print 2 (gold), cut:
- ✦ 4—2" x 3½" rectangles for 9" blocks
- ✦ 4—1½" x 2½" rectangles for 6" blocks

From medium/dark print 3 (red), cut:
- ✦ 1—3½" square for 9" blocks
- ✦ 1—2½" square for 6" blocks

From light print, cut:
- ✦ 2—4" squares for 9" blocks
- ✦ 4—2" x 3½" rectangles for 9" blocks
- ✦ 2—3" squares for 6" blocks
- ✦ 4—1½" x 2½" rectangles for 6" blocks

Sewing Instructions

1. Draw a diagonal line from corner to corner on the wrong side of the 4" light print squares for the 9" blocks OR 3" light print squares for the 6" blocks. With right sides together, layer the light print square on top of the olive green print square. Sew a ¼" from both sides of the drawn line, then cut apart on the drawn line. Press seams toward the olive green print. Trim the unit to 3½" square for the 9" blocks OR 2½" square for the 6" blocks. Repeat to make a total of four half-square triangle units per block. Set aside.

2. Draw a diagonal line from corner to corner on the wrong side of the 2" olive green print squares for the 9" blocks OR 1½" olive green print squares for the 6" blocks. Layer an olive green print square on top of a light print rectangle and sew on the drawn line. Trim the outer portion of the olive green print square as shown below and press the rest of it back. Repeat with another olive green print square on the opposite side of the light print rectangle. Repeat to create a total of four Flying Geese units per block.

3. Sew a gold print rectangle to a unit from the previous step. Press seam toward the gold print. Repeat to create a total of four units per block.

 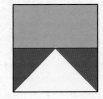

4. To complete the block, sew together the units from step 3 and step 1 to a 3½" red print square for the 9" blocks OR 2½" red print square for the 6" blocks. Press the seams toward the half-square triangle units or center square.

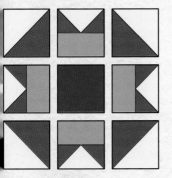

5. Repeat steps 1–4 to create a total of 4—9" blocks and 9—6" blocks.

BLOCK 6

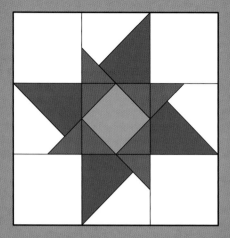

Cutting Instructions

From medium/dark print 1 (red), cut:
- ✦ 2—4" squares for 9" blocks
- ✦ 2—3" squares for 6" blocks

From medium/dark print 2 (brown), cut:
- ✦ 8—2" squares for 9" blocks
- ✦ 8—1½" squares for 6" blocks

From medium/dark print 3 (blue), cut:
- ✦ 1—3½" square for 9" blocks
- ✦ 1—2½" square for 6" blocks

From light print, cut:
- ✦ 2—4" squares for 9" blocks
- ✦ 4—3½" squares for 9" blocks
- ✦ 2—3" squares for 6" blocks
- ✦ 4—2½" squares for 6" blocks

Sewing Instructions

1. Draw a diagonal line from corner to corner on the wrong side of the 4" light print squares for the 9" blocks OR 3" light print squares for the 6" blocks. Layer a light print square on top of a red print square, then sew on the drawn line. Cut apart on the drawn line. Press seams toward the red print. Trim the unit to 3½" square for the 9" blocks OR 2½" for the 6" blocks. Repeat to create a total of four half-square triangle units per block. Set aside.

2. Draw a diagonal line on the wrong side of the 2" brown print squares for the 9" blocks OR 1½" brown print squares for the 6" blocks. Layer the brown print square in the lower left-hand corner of one of the units from the previous step, then sew on the drawn line. Trim the outer portion of the brown print square, then press it back. Repeat to create a total of four units per block.

3. Draw a diagonal line from corner to corner on the wrong side of the remaining brown print squares. Layer a brown print square on top of a larger 3½" blue print square for the 9" blocks OR 2½" blue print square for the 6" blocks. Sew on the drawn line, then trim the outer portion of the brown print square and press it back. Repeat in the opposite diagonal corner of the larger blue print square as shown below. (Sew opposite sides rather than going around the block, which can distort the piece.) Repeat for the remaining two corners of the blue print square.

4. To complete the block, sew together the unit from the previous step and the four units from step 2 to the four 3½" light print squares for the 9" blocks OR 2½" light print squares for the 6" blocks. Press seams toward the units from step 2 or center square.

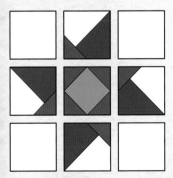

5. Repeat steps 1–4 to create a total of 4—9" blocks and 9—6" blocks.

Block Assembly

1. For each of the six block designs, sew together four 9" blocks to create an 18½" square block. Press seams open.

2. For each of the six block designs, sew together nine 6" blocks to create an 18½" square block. Press seams open.

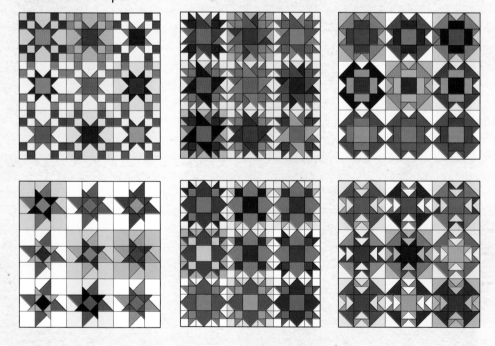

Quilt Center

Referring to the quilt assembly diagram on page 25, lay out the 12 blocks and sashing strips. Join the blocks and sashing strips into four rows of three blocks and two sashing strips each. Complete the quilt center by joining those four rows with the 3−2" x 57½" long sashing strips that separate the rows, being careful to match up the edges of the blocks with each other. Since sashing strips separate the block rows, you will need to take extra care in doing this step.

Quilt Assembly Diagram

3. Using a variety of colors, sew a tota of 190 units from step 2, following the instructions in the previous step and making sure the larger light/cream print background areas are all on the same side. Press the seams in the same direction or open.

4. Sew together 54 units from the previous step to create a side border strip. Repeat to create a second side stri

5. Sew together 41 units from step 3 to create a top border strip. Repeat to create a bottom strip.

6. To make the border cornerstones, ma a diagonal line from corner to corner or the wrong side of two 2" medium/dark print squares. Layer the square on top of the end of a light/cream background rectangle, then sew on the drawn line and press it back. Repeat to create a total of eight units.

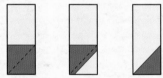

7. Sew a medium/dark print square to the unit from the previous step. Sew another strip from step 6 to a 4¼" crea print square, then join all those units to create a border cornerstone square. Repeat to create a total of four border cornerstone squares.

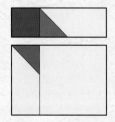

Outer Border

To make sure your outer pieced border fits your quilt top and inner border perfectly, Jill suggests that you create the outer pieced border prior to sewing your inner border to the quilt.

1. On the wrong side of the 2" light/cream print background squares, draw a diagonal line from corner to corner.

2. Layer a marked light/cream print square on top of one end of the medium/dark print rectangle and sew on the marked line. Trim the outer section of the square as shown in the second diagram below. On the wrong side of the 2" x 2¼" light/cream print background rectangles, mark a diagonal line as shown in the fourth diagram below, then turn up one corner on the wrong side and press. (NOTE: This light rectangular end will be positioned toward the outside of the border to allow more room to apply your binding without the risk of cutting off any colored print points.) Sew on the pressed line.

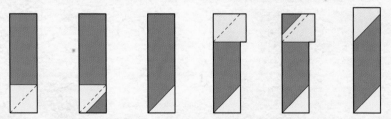

Finishing the Quilt

1. Measure your top and bottom outer border strip from end to end and measure your quilt top through the middle from side to side. Subtract the quilt top measurement from the border measurement and divide that number by two and add ½". This is the width you will need to cut your side inner border strips. Referring to the quilt assembly diagram, sew these strips to the sides of the quilt center. Press seams toward the border.

2. Measure your side outer border strip and the quilt top through the center from top to bottom. Subtract the quilt top measurement from the border measurement and divide that number by two and add ½". This is the width you will need to cut your top and bottom inner border strips. Sew a border cornerstone to each end of one of these strips, being careful that the larger portion of the light/cream print background faces the outer edge of the quilt. Repeat for the other strip. Referring to the quilt assembly diagram, sew these strips to the sides of the quilt top. Press seams toward the border.

3. Sandwich the quilt top, batting, and backing; baste. Quilt, then bind.

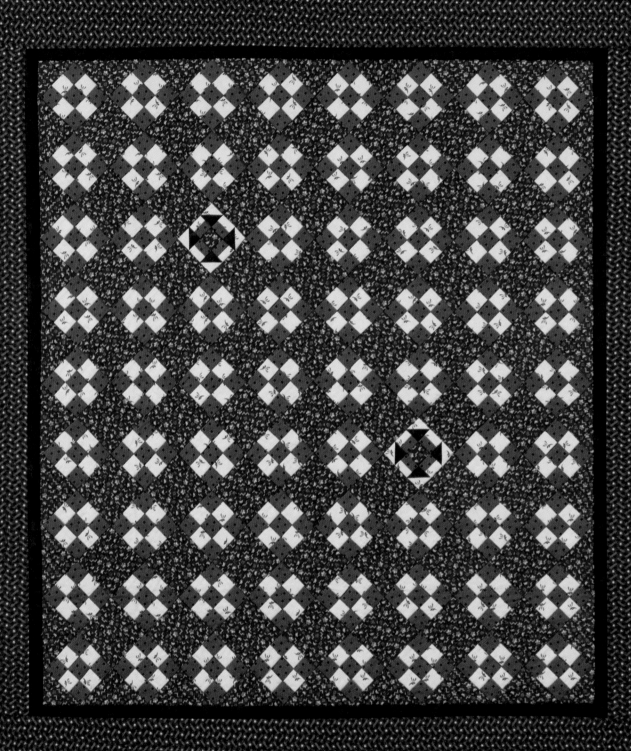

Finished quilt size: 41¾" x 46"   **Finished block size:** 3" x 3"

Designed by Jill Shaulis
Quilted by Janet Graves

I love working with small, traditional blocks, and I like to throw in a little surprise. Two Churn Dash blocks add that unexpected element to this cozy quilt dressed in a classic palette of brown and blue.

Fabric Requirements

- ¾ yard brown print for Nine-Patch and Churn Dash blocks
- ⅔ yard tan print for Nine-Patch and Churn Dash blocks
- 1 yard blue multi print for setting squares, setting triangles, and corner triangles
- ¼ yard black print for Churn Dash blocks and inner border
- 1 yard blue/black print for outer border and binding
- 1⅜ yard fabric of choice for backing

Cutting Instructions

From brown print, cut:
- 15—1½" strips the width of fabric for Nine-Patch blocks
- 8—1" x 1½" rectangles for Churn Dash blocks

From tan print, cut:
- 12—1½" strips the width of fabric for Nine-Patch blocks
- 8—1" x 1½" rectangles for Churn Dash blocks
- 4—2" squares for Churn Dash blocks

From blue multi print, cut:
- 2—1½" squares for Churn Dash blocks
- 56—3½" squares for setting squares
- 8—6" squares, then cut each twice diagonally from corner to corner for setting triangles

- 2—4½" squares, then cut each once diagonally from corner to corner for corner triangles

From black print, cut:
- 4—2" squares for Churn Dash blocks
- 2—1¼" x 39" side strips for inner border
- 2—1¼" x 36¼" top and bottom strips for inner border

From blue/black print, cut:
- 2—3¼" x 40½" side strips for outer border
- 2—3¼" x 41¾" top and bottom strips for outer border
- 5—3" strips the width of fabric for binding

Sewing Instructions

Nine-Patch Blocks

1. Using 12 brown print strips and six tan print strips, make six strip sets like the one shown below. Press seams toward the brown print. Then sub-cut the strip sets into a total of 140—1½"-wide segments.

2. Using six tan print strips and three brown print strips, make three strip sets like the one shown below. Press seams toward the brown print. Then sub-cut the strips into a total of 70—1½"-wide segments.

3. Using two of the segments from step 1 and one of the segments from step 2, make a Nine-Patch block, which should measure 3½" square. Repeat to create a total of 70 Nine-Patch blocks. Set aside.

Churn Dash Blocks

1. Sew a tan print rectangle to a brown print rectangle. Press seam toward the brown print. Repeat to make a total of eight units.

2. With right sides together, layer a tan print square on top of a black print square, draw a diagonal line on the wrong side of the tan print square, then sew a ¼" from both sides of the drawn line. Repeat to make a total of eight half-square triangle units.

3. Sew four units from step 1, four units from step 2, and a 1½" multi-blue print square to create a Churn Dash block. Repeat to create a total of two Churn Dash blocks, which should measure 3½" square. Press seams toward the tan/brown print sections.

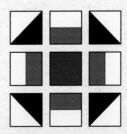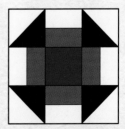

Quilt Assembly

1. Referring to the quilt assembly diagram on page 33, lay out the Nine-Patch blocks, the Churn Dash blocks, the blue print setting squares, the blue print setting triangles, and blue print corner triangles. (NOTE: The setting and corner triangles are oversized and will be trimmed to size later.)

2. Referring to the quilt assembly diagram, sew the units from step 1 into rows, then join the rows to complete the quilt center. Press seams toward the multi-blue print setting squares and setting triangles.

3. Trim the setting and corner triangles to ⅜" from the edges of the blocks so that the blocks will appear to float within the inner border.

4. Referring to the quilt assembly diagram, sew the 2—1¼" x 39" inner border strips to the sides of the quilt center.

5. Sew the 2—1¼" x 36¼" inner border strips to the top and bottom of the quilt center.

6. Referring to the quilt assembly diagram, sew the 2—3¼" x 40½" outer border strips to the sides of the quilt top.

7. Sew the 2—3¼" x 41¾" outer border strips to the top and bottom of the quilt top.

8. Sandwich the quilt top, batting, and backing; baste. Quilt as desired, then bind.

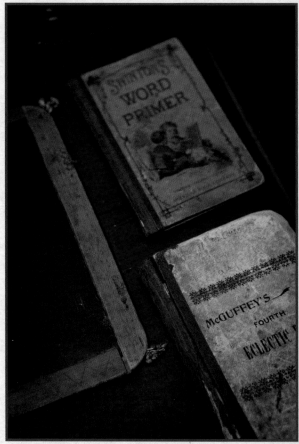

Quilt Assembly Diagram

Finished quilt size: 67" x 77"   **Finished block size:** 5" x 5"

Designed by Vicki Olsen
Quilted by Dan Kolbe

I love traditional quilt block patterns and how today's reproduction prints bring them to life. While searching my stash of quilt blocks that didn't make it into past quilts, I spotted a Snowball block and Nine-Patch Variation block and thought they would make the perfect companions for a new quilt project. As I sketched my design, the secondary pattern emerged and it really came to life in the finished quilt.

Fabric Requirements

+ 5⅛ yards large blue print for blocks, outer border, and binding
+ 1⅓ yards cream print for Nine-Patch Variation blocks and Snowball blocks
+ ⅞ yard brown dot for Nine-Patch Variation blocks and inner border
+ 4 yards fabric of choice for backing

Cutting Instructions

From large blue print, cut:
+ 11 — 5½" strips the width of fabric, then sub-cut them into 71 — 5½" squares for Snowball blocks
+ 12 — 3½" strips the width of fabric, then sub-cut 6 of them into 144 — 1½" x 3½" rectangles for Nine-Patch Variation blocks (set the remaining 6 strips aside for later use with the Nine-Patch Variation blocks)
+ 8 — 5½" strips the width of fabric, then join and cut them into 4 — 5½" x 67½" strips for outer border
+ 8 — 3" strips the width of fabric for binding

From cream print, cut:
+ 38 — 1½" strips the width of fabric, then sub-cut 11 of them into 284 — 1½" squares for Snowball blocks (set the remaining 27 strips aside for later use with the Nine-Patch Variation blocks)

From brown dot, cut:
+ 4 — 1½" strips the width of fabric for Nine-Patch Variation blocks
+ 3 — 1½" strips the width of fabric, then join and cut them into 2 — 1½" x 65½" side strips for inner border
+ 3 strips the width of fabric, then join and cut them into 2 — 1½" x 57½" top and bottom strips for inner border

Sewing Instructions

Snowball Blocks

1. On the wrong side of 284—1½" cream print squares, draw a diagonal line from corner to corner.

2. Layer a 1½" cream print square on top of a corner of the 5½" large blue print square and stitch on the drawn line. To reduce bulk, you can trim the outer corner of the light square as shown in the second diagram. Repeat this step for the remaining three corners of the 5½" square.

3. Repeat step 2 to make a total of 71 Snowball blocks.

Nine-Patch Variation Blocks

1. Using 12—1½" x WOF cream print strips and 6—1½" x WOF brown dot strips, make six strip sets like the one shown below. Press seams toward the brown dot fabric. Then sub-cut the strip sets into a total of 144—1½"-wide segments.

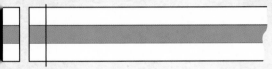

2. Using 3—1½" x WOF cream print strips and 6—1½" x WOF brown dot strips, make three strip sets like the one shown below. Press seams toward the brown dot fabric. Then sub-cut the strip sets into a total of 72—1½"-wide segments.

3. Make 72 Nine-Patch blocks with the segments cut from steps 1 and 2.

4. Using 12—1½" x WOF cream print strips and 6—3½" x WOF large blue print strips, make six strips sets like the one shown below. Press seams toward the large blue print. Then sub-cut the strip sets into a total of 144—1½"-wide segments.

5. Sew the 1½" x 3½" blue print rectangles to the sides of each Nine-Patch unit. Press seams toward the rectangles. Sew two units from step 4 to the top and bottom of each Nine-Patch unit to complete the Nine-Patch Variation blocks.

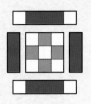

Quilt Assembly

1. Referring to the quilt assembly diagram on page 38, lay out all the Nine-Patch Variation blocks and Snowball blocks, alternating them into 13 rows of 11 blocks each, to create the quilt center, which should measure 55½" x 65½".

2. Referring to the quilt assembly diagram, sew the 2—1½" x 65½" brown dot inner border strips to the sides of the quilt center. Then sew the 2—1½" x 57½" brown dot inner border strips to the top and bottom of the quilt top.

3. Referring to the quilt assembly diagram, sew 2—5½" x 67½" blue print outer border strips to the sides of the quilt top. Then sew the remaining 2—5½" x 67½" blue print outer border strips to the top and bottom of the quilt top.

4. Sandwich the quilt top, batting, and backing; baste. Quilt as desired, then bind.

Quilt Assembly Diagram

BABY STEPS

Finished quilt size: 19" x 19"   **Finished block size:** 2½" x 2½"

Designed by Vicki Olsen
Quilted by Dan Kolbe

A scrappy twist on my larger Stepping Stones quilt, this smaller rendition spotlights blocks made with a handy 5" charm pack of fabrics.

Fabric Requirements

✦ 1 charm pack for Snowball blocks, Nine-Patch Variation blocks, and inner pieced border OR 13 medium/dark 5" squares and 10–12 light 5" squares
✦ ½ yard black print for outer border and binding
✦ ⅝ yard fabric of choice for backing

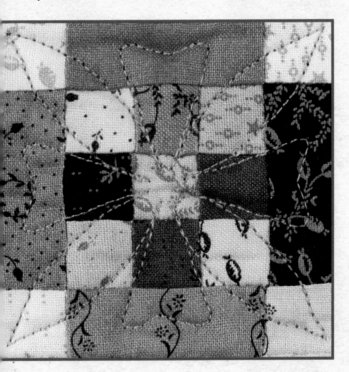

Cutting Instructions

From *each* of 13 dark/medium charms, cut:
✦ 1–3" square for Snowball blocks
✦ 4–1" x 2" rectangles for Nine-Patch Variation blocks and inner pieced border (12 of these will be used for the inner pieced border)

From leftovers of the 13 dark/medium charms above, cut:
✦ 48–1" squares for Nine-Patch Variation blocks
✦ 2–1½" squares for corner half-square triangles in inner pieced border

From 10-12 light charms, cut:
✦ 8–1" x 4" rectangles for inner pieced border
✦ 168–1" squares for Snowball blocks, Nine-Patch Variation blocks, and inner pieced border (52 are for the Snowball blocks, 108 for the Nine-Patch Variation blocks, and 8 for the inner border)
✦ 2–1½" squares for corner half-square triangles in inner pieced border

From black print, cut:
✦ 2–3" x 14" side strips for outer border
✦ 2–3" x 19" top and bottom strips for outer border
✦ 3–3" strips the width of fabric for binding

Sewing Instructions

Snowball Block

1. On the back of the 52–1" light print squares, draw a diagonal line from corner to corner. Then place a 1" light print square on top of a corner of the 3" dark print square and stitch on the drawn line. To reduce bulk, you can trim the outer corner of the light square as shown in the second square below. (However, if your light fabric is very light, you may not want to do this because the dark print underneath might show through.) Repeat this step for the remaining three corners of the 3" square.

2. Repeat step 1 to create a total of 13 Snowball blocks.

Nine-Patch Blocks

Using 5–1" light print squares and 4–1" dark/
medium print squares, make a Nine-Patch block.
Press seams toward the dark print when possible.
Repeat to make a total of 12 Nine-Patch blocks. Set
aside for now.

Quilt Center

1. To create the Nine-Patch Variation block, you
will sew an outer layer of four rectangles and
four squares around each Nine-Patch block. To
determine the appropriate colored dark/medium
rectangles to sew to the Nine-Patch blocks so that
they match the fabrics in the adjoining Snowball
blocks, lay out all the Snowball blocks and Nine-
Patch blocks, referring to the quilt assembly
diagram on page 43. **(NOTE: At this point, the Nine-
Patch blocks would not yet include the outer layer
of rectangles and squares that surrounds them as
shown in the quilt assembly diagram—these are
the units you are color-coordinating in this step.)**

2. Sew the appropriate dark/medium print
rectangle to each side of the Nine-Patch blocks.
Press seams toward the rectangle. Then sew a light
print square to each end of 24 dark/medium print
rectangles. Press seams toward the rectangle. Sew
the appropriate strips containing the two squares
and rectangle to the top and bottom of the middle
row of the following diagram to complete each of
the 12 Nine-Patch Variation blocks.

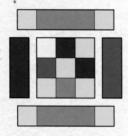

3. Referring to the quilt assembly diagram on
page 43, sew together the Snowball blocks and
Nine-Patch Variation blocks to create the quilt
center. Press seams toward the Nine-Patch Variation
blocks when possible or press the seams open.

Pieced Inner Border

1. With right sides together, layer a 1½" light
square on top of a 1½" dark/medium print square.
Draw a diagonal line from corner to corner on the
wrong side of the light print square and stitch
¼" from each side of the drawn line. Cut on the
drawn line. Press seams toward the dark print or
press them open. Trim the units to measure 1"
square. Repeat to make a total of four half-square
triangle units.

2. Referring to the inner border in the quilt
assembly diagram, sew the following units in
this order to create a side border strip: a 1" light
print square, a 1" x 2" rectangle that matches the
adjoining Snowball block, a 1" x 4" light print
rectangle, a 1" x 2" rectangle that matches the
adjoining Snowball block, a 1" x 4" light print
rectangle, a 1" x 2" rectangle that matches the
adjoining Snowball block, and finally, a 1" light
print square. Repeat to create a second side
border strip, then sew the two strips to the sides
of the quilt center. Press both seams toward the
pieced borders.

3. Following the instructions in the previous
step, sew the top and bottom inner pieced borders,
adding a half-square triangle unit to each end
with the dark triangle facing out. Then sew the
strips to the top and bottom of the quilt top.

Outer Border

1. Referring to the quilt assembly diagram, sew
the 2–3" x 14" outer border strips to the sides of
the quilt top. Press seams toward the border.

2. Sew the 2–3" x 19" outer border strips to
the top and bottom of the quilt top. Press seams
toward the border.

3. Sandwich the quilt top, batting, and backing;
baste. Quilt, then bind.

Quilt Assembly Diagram

DANCING STARS

Finished size: 24½" x 31½"

Designed and quilted by Jill Shaulis

I love creating designs that dance across a quilt. Inspired by my fondness for star block designs, I created that effect with a repeating pattern of seven stars in this wall hanging. Make your own star-studded galaxy with this design that uses Flying Geese units and various colored strips to create the interlocking pattern of stars.

Fabric Requirements

+ ¼ yard each of red print, green print, blue print, and brown print for stars (we added scraps in each color for more variety)
+ 1⅛ yards light print for background and border
+ ⅜ yard red print for binding
+ ⅞ yard fabric of choice for backing

Cutting Instructions

From red print, cut:
+ 56—1½" squares for stars
+ 7—2½" squares for stars

From green print, cut:
+ 56—1½" squares for stars
+ 7—2½" squares for stars

From blue print, cut:
+ 56—1½" squares for stars
+ 7—2½" squares for stars

From brown print, cut:
+ 56—1½" squares for stars
+ 7—2½" squares for stars

From light print, cut:
+ 112—1½" x 2½" strips for background
+ 2—2½" x 3½" strips for background
+ 1—2½" x 8½" strip for background
+ 18—1½" x 4½" strips for background
+ 12—1½" x 2½" strips for background
+ 6—1½" x 9½" strips for background
+ 12—1½" x 3½" strips for background
+ 2—2½" x 9½" strips for background
+ 2—1½" x 24½" strips for background
+ 2—1½" x 29½" strips for background
+ 28—1½" squares for background

From red print, cut:
+ 4—3" strips the width of fabric for binding

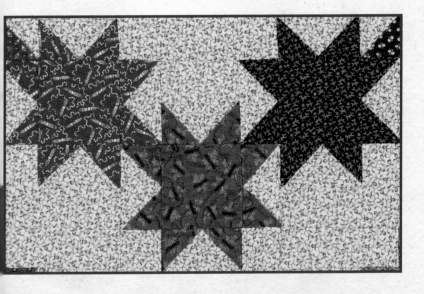

Sewing Instructions

Flying Geese Units

1. Draw a diagonal line on the wrong side of all the 1½" red, green, blue, and brown squares.

2. With right sides together, layer a 1½" red print square on top of a 1½" x 2½" light print rectangle and stitch on the drawn line. Trim away the outer corner of the red square, leaving the light print rectangle below intact to provide a squared edge to stitch the adjoining pieces to later. Press back the red print triangle of the unit. Repeat this step with another red print square on the opposite side of the rectangle to complete the Flying Geese unit. Repeat this step to make a total of 28 red Flying Geese units.

3. Repeat step 2 to make a total of 28 green Flying Geese units, 28 blue Flying Geese units, and 28 brown Flying Geese units.

Quilt Assembly

1. Referring to the quilt assembly diagram on page 48, sew together the Flying Geese units and the light print strips to create the quilt top. Press seams open or toward the star centers.

2. Referring to the quilt assembly diagram, sew the 2−1½" x 29½" side border strips to the quilt center.

3. Referring to the quilt assembly diagram, sew the 2−1½" x 24½" top and bottom border strips to the quilt top.

4. Sandwich the quilt top, batting, and backing; baste. Quilt as desired, then bind.

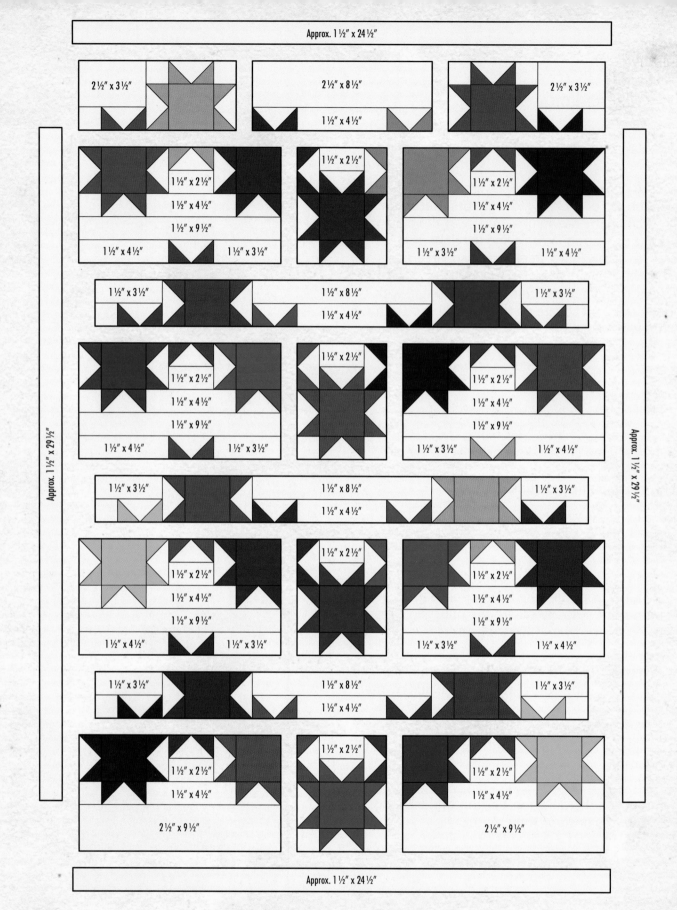

Quilt Assembly Diagram

All dimensions above are finished sizes. Small background squares above are 1" x 1" finished.

Finished quilt size: 20½" x 24½"   **Finished block size:** 4½" x 5½"

Designed and quilted
by Jill Shaulis

The Courthouse Steps block is so versatile. Using dark 1800s reproduction fabrics, I transformed 16 of them into a multicolored design accented with a basket of wool flowers so abundant that they spill over the boundaries of their background block.

Fabric Requirements

- ⅛ yard each of 5 blue prints for Courthouse Steps blocks
- ⅛ yard each of 6 purple prints for Courthouse Steps blocks
- ⅛ yard each of 5 red prints for Courthouse Steps blocks
- ⅛ yard each of 4 brown prints for Courthouse Steps blocks
- ⅛ yard each of 5 green prints for Courthouse Steps blocks
- ⅛ yard each of 5 black prints for Courthouse Steps blocks
- ⅛ yard of 1 cream print for Courthouse Steps block
- 2½" x 5" brown wool for basket
- 2" square gold wool for star
- 3½" x 4" green wool for stems and leaves
- 3½" x 4" red wool for flowers
- 2½" square each of two blue/teal wools for flowers and star accent
- 2½" x 3½" purple wool for flowers
- 1½" x 3" brown/gold wool for blue/teal flower center and bases of red flowers
- 2" square gold wool for purple flower centers
- ⅝ yard black print for block centers, border, and binding
- ⅔ yard fabric of choice for backing
- ¼ yard Steam-A-Seam fusible web
- Valdani thread to match wools

Cutting Instructions

From *each* of 5 blue prints, 6 purple prints, 5 red prints, 4 brown prints, 5 green prints, and 5 black prints, cut:

- 2–1" x 2" rectangles for Courthouse Steps blocks
- 2–1" x 3" rectangles for Courthouse Steps blocks
- 2–1" x 4" rectangles for Courthouse Steps blocks
- 2–1" x 5" rectangles for Courthouse Steps blocks

From cream print, cut:

- 5–1" x 2" rectangles for Courthouse Steps blocks
- 4–1" x 3" rectangles for Courthouse Steps blocks
- 4–1" x 4" rectangles for Courthouse Steps blocks
- 4–1" x 5" rectangles for Courthouse Steps blocks

From black print, cut:

- 15–1" x 2" rectangles for Courthouse Steps block centers
- 2–1¾" x 22½" side strips for border
- 2–1¾" x 21" top and bottom strips for border
- 3–3" strips the width of fabric for binding

From various wools listed in the **Fabric Requirements**, cut the basket, star, star accent, flowers, flower centers, flower bases, leaves, and stems on page 54.

Sewing Instructions

1. Referring to the diagram below for rectangle placement and the quilt assembly diagram on page 53 for color cues, lay out the strips needed for the first block (in the top left corner of the quilt). Sew the appropriate colored rectangles to each side of the black center rectangle. Press seams away from the black rectangle. Add the appropriate colored rectangle to the top and bottom of the previous unit and press the seams away from the block center. Continue sewing rectangles around the block until all the sides are complete.

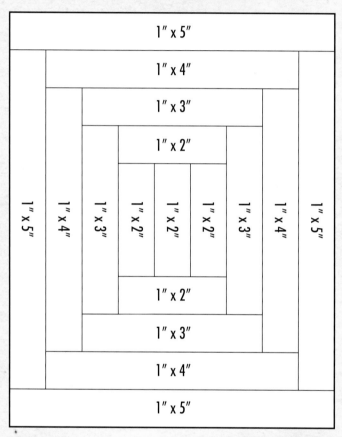

2. Referring to the diagram in the previous step for rectangle placement and the quilt assembly diagram for color cues, repeat step 1 for the remaining 15 blocks. Note: You will make one block with the cream print rectangles only.

3. Referring to the quilt assembly diagram, sew together the four rows of four blocks each. Join the rows to create the quilt center.

4. Following the fusible web manufacturer's instructions, fuse the wool pieces to the fusible web. Referring to the photo on page 50 for placement, appliqué the wool pieces to the quilt top using a blanket stitch.

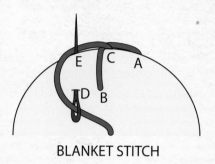

BLANKET STITCH

5. Referring to the quilt assembly diagram, sew the 2—1¾" x 22½" black print border strips to the sides of the quilt center.

6. Referring to the quilt assembly diagram, sew the 2—1¾" x 21" black print border strips to the top and bottom of the quilt top.

7. Sandwich the quilt top, batting, and backing; baste. Quilt as desired, then bind.

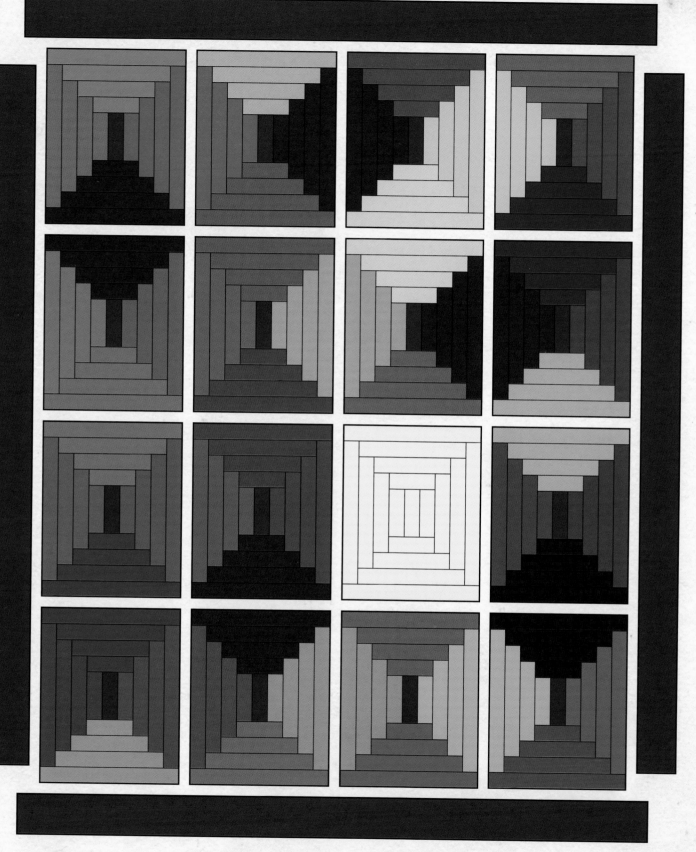

Quilt Assembly Diagram

Pattern is already reversed for use with fusible web

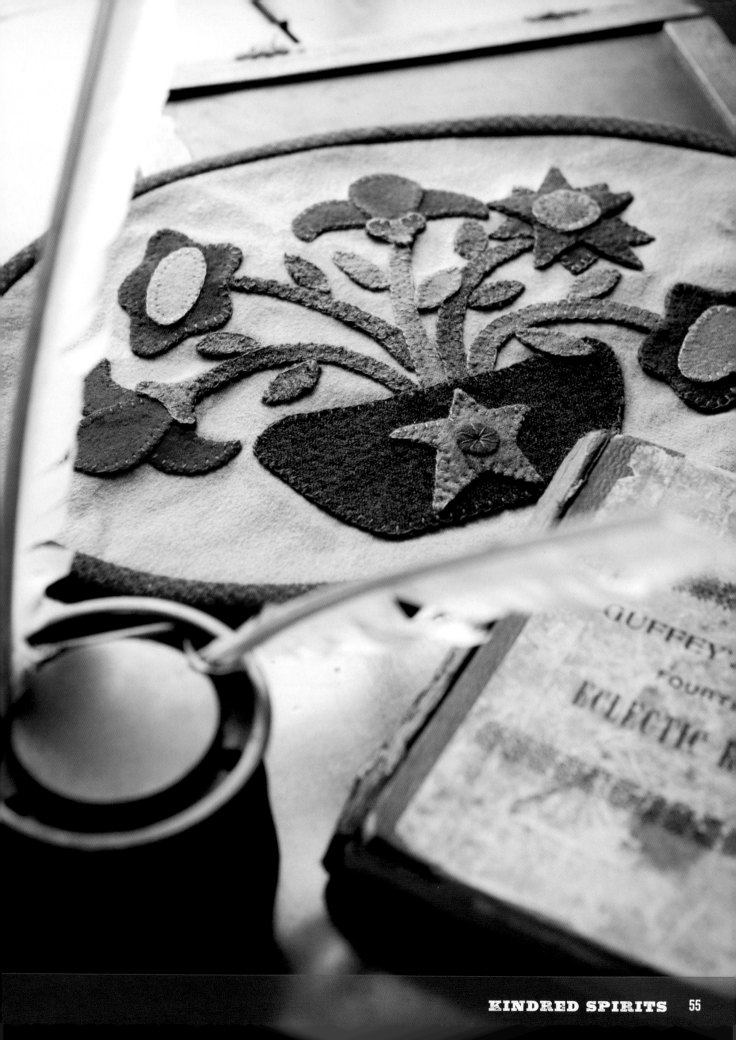

SIMPLY JOYFUL

Finished size: Approximately 9½" x 13½"

Designed by Jill Shaulis

A delightful twist on the Joyful Abundance wall hanging on page 50, this welcoming table mat is abloom with a colorful medley of wool flowers. Gather some of your wool scraps to create your own simply joyful version!

Fabric Requirements

- 3½" x 6" brown wool for basket
- 2½" square gold wool for star
- 5" x 6" green wool for stems and leaves of teal flower, left red flower, and left purple flower
- 4" square green wool for stem and leaves of center red flower and right purple flower
- 4" x 5" red wool for flowers
- 3" x 4½" purple wool for flowers
- 3" square each of two blue/teal wools for flowers and star accent

- 2" x 3" brown/gold wool for purple flower centers
- 1½" x 3½" brown wool for bases of red flowers and blue/teal flower center
- ⅓ yard camel-color flannel for table mat background front and back
- Valdani threads to match wools
- ½ yard Steam-A-Seam fusible web
- 15" square red flannel for bias binding

Cutting Instructions

From various wools listed in the **Fabric Requirements**, cut the basket, star, star accent, flowers, flower centers, flower bases, leaves, stems, and two ovals for the mat front and back on pages 58 and 59.

Sewing Instructions

1. Referring to the fusible web manufacturer instructions, fuse the wool pieces to the fusible web.

2. Referring to the photo on page 56 for placement, appliqué the wool pieces to the background oval with a blanket stitch.

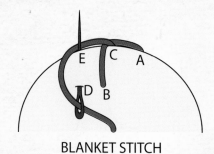

BLANKET STITCH

3. Apply Steam-A-Seam to the wrong side of the appliquéd oval. With wrong sides together, layer the front appliquéd oval and back oval, then fuse them together. This will help the piece lay nice and flat. Bind the table mat with bias binding.

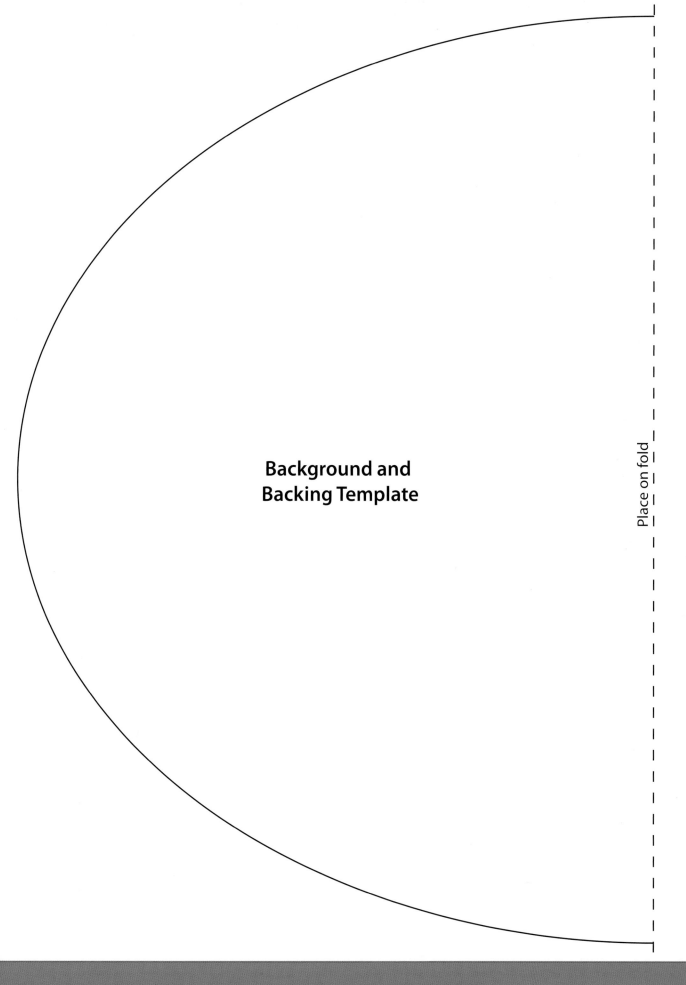

**Background and
Backing Template**

Place on fold

THREE OF A KIND

Designed by Jill Shaulis   Quilted by Dan Kolbe

A single block design makes a dazzling repeat performance in this inviting table runner. I made one with 9" blocks and a smaller version with 6" blocks. For a fun twist, swap out this block design with one or more from our sampler quilt on page 10.

Large Table Runner

Large table runner finished size: 18¼" x 43¾"   **Large table runner finished block size:** 9" x 9"

Small Table Runner

Small table runner finished size: 12" x 29"   **Small table runner finished block size:** 6" x 6"

Fabric Requirements

LARGE TABLE RUNNER:

✦ ⅝ yard brown print for blocks, setting triangles, and corner triangles
✦ ⅞ yard red floral for blocks, border, and binding
✦ ⅛ yard red print for blocks
✦ ⅓ yard tan print for blocks
✦ ⅝ yard fabric of choice for backing

SMALL TABLE RUNNER:

✦ ⅜ yard brown print for blocks, setting triangles, and corner triangles
✦ ⅝ yard blue print for blocks, border, and binding
✦ ⅛ yard black print for blocks
✦ ¼ yard cream print for blocks
✦ ½ yard fabric of choice for backing

Cutting Instructions

LARGE TABLE RUNNER:

From brown print, cut:
✦ 12—2½" squares for blocks
✦ 1—14" square, then cut it twice diagonally from corner to corner to yield a total of four setting triangles

✦ 2—7¼" squares, then cut each once diagonally from corner to corner to yield a total of four corner triangles

From red floral, cut:
✦ 12—2" squares for blocks
✦ 3—3½" squares for blocks
✦ 2—3" x 13¼" strips for border
✦ 2—3" x 43¾" strips for border
✦ 4—3" strips the width of fabric for binding

From red print, cut:
✦ 6—4¼" squares for blocks

From tan print, cut:
✦ 12—2½" squares for blocks
✦ 12—2" squares for blocks
✦ 6—4¼" squares for blocks

SMALL TABLE RUNNER:

From brown print, cut:
✦ 12—2" squares for blocks
✦ 1—9¾" square, then cut it twice diagonally from corner to corner to yield a total of four setting triangles

✦ 2—5⅛" squares, then cut each once diagonally from corner to corner to yield a total of four corner triangles

From blue print, cut:
✦ 12—1½" squares for blocks
✦ 3—2½" squares for blocks
✦ 2—2" x 9" side strips for border
✦ 2—2" x 29" top and bottom strips for border
✦ 3—3" strips the width of fabric for binding

From black print, cut:
✦ 6—3¼" squares for blocks

From cream print, cut:
✦ 12—2" squares for blocks
✦ 12—1½" squares for blocks
✦ 6—3¼" squares for blocks

Sewing Instructions

LARGE TABLE RUNNER

1. Draw a diagonal line from corner to corner on the wrong side of the 2½" tan print squares. With right sides together, layer the tan print square on top of a 2½" brown print square. Sew a ¼" from both sides of the drawn line. Cut on the drawn line, then press open the half-square triangle units, which should measure 2" square. Press seams toward the brown print. Repeat this step to create a total of 24 half-square triangle units.

2. Referring to the following diagram, sew two half-square triangle units from step 1 to a 2" tan print square and 2" red floral square to create the following unit. Repeat to create a total of 12 of these units.

3. On the wrong side of the 4¼" tan print squares, draw a diagonal line from corner to corner. With right sides together, layer a tan print square on top of a 4¼" red print square, then sew a ¼" from both sides of the drawn line. Cut apart on the drawn line, then press open the half-square triangle units.

Press seams toward the red print. Cut the half-square triangle units in half as shown below.

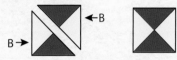

4. Referring to the following diagram, sew two B units from step 3 to create an Hourglass unit. Repeat with two A units. If necessary, trim the unit to measure 3½" square. Repeat steps 3 and 4 to create a total of 12 units.

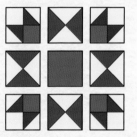

5. Referring to the following diagram, sew four units from step 4, four units from step 2, and a 3½" red floral square to complete a block. Repeat to make a total of three blocks.

6. Referring to the following diagram, sew together the three blocks, four setting triangles, and four corner triangles to create the table runner center.

7. Referring to the following diagram, sew the 2–3" x 13¼" border strips to the sides of the table runner. Then sew the 2–3" x 43¾" border strips to the top and bottom of the table runner.

SMALL TABLE RUNNER

1. Draw a diagonal line from corner to corner on the wrong side of the 2" cream print squares. With right sides together, layer the cream print square on top of a 2" brown print square. Sew a ¼" from both sides of the drawn line. Cut on the drawn line, then press open the half-square triangle units, which should measure 1½" square. Press seams toward the brown print. Repeat this step to create a total of 24 half-square triangle units.

2. Referring to the following diagram, sew together the two half-square triangle units from step 1, a 1½" cream print square, and a 1½" blue print square to create the following unit. Repeat to create a total of 12 of these units.

3. On the wrong side of the 3¼" cream print squares, draw a diagonal line from corner to corner. With right sides together, layer a cream print square on top of a 3¼" black print square, then sew a ¼" from both sides of the drawn line. Cut apart on the drawn line, then press open the half-square triangle units. Press seams toward the black print. Then cut the half-square triangle units in half as shown below.

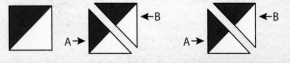

4. Sew two B units from step 3 to create an Hourglass unit, which should measure 2½" square. Repeat with two A units. Repeat steps 3 and 4 to create a total of 12 Hourglass units.

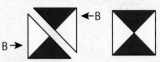

5. Referring to the following diagram, sew four units from step 4, four units from step 2, and a 2½" blue print square to complete the block. Repeat to make a total of three blocks.

6. Referring to the following diagram, sew together the three blocks, four setting triangles, and four corner triangles to create the table runner center.

7. Referring to the following diagram, sew the 2—2" x 9" border strips to the sides of the table runner. Then sew the 2—2" x 29" border strips to the top and bottom of the table runner.

8. Sandwich the table runner top, batting, and backing; baste. Quilt as desired, then bind.

PICKLE DISH

Designed by Jill Shaulis

For many years, I thought hexagons were only appropriate for reproduction 1930s Grandmother's Flower Garden quilts—that was, until I saw a stunning 19th-century version of this design called "Pickle Dish." I loved the color and fabrics, and since I'm happiest when my hands are busy, I quickly took to the English paper piecing method of constructing the hexagons. I used two different size hexagons to create a large and small version of this project. Instead of quilting my projects, I opted to display them in handmade frames made of old barn wood.

Large Pickle Dish

Large version finished size:
19½" x 25" (not including frame)

½"

Template

Small Pickle Dish

Small version finished size:
9¾" x 14¼" (not including frame)

¼"

Template

Fabric Requirements

This project requires a border to frame it, however the border is not visible in the finished project. Jill used ½" hexagons for the large version and ¼" ones for the small version. Yardage requirements for the small project are listed in parentheses below. Jill used pre-cut hexagons by Paper Pieces (available at quilt shops) because they are accurate and can be used several times.

- ✦ ½ yard tan print for hexagons (¼ yard)
- ✦ 1⅛ yards assorted dark/medium prints for hexagons (½ yard)
- ✦ ⅓ yard fabric of choice for border (¼ yard)

Cutting Instructions

Templates do not include a seam allowance. The cutting instructions for the small version of this project are listed in parentheses below.

From tan print, cut:
- ✦ 9—1⅝" strips the width of fabric, then sub-cut the strips into 206—1⅝ squares for tan hexagons (for small version, cut 6—1" strips, then sub-cut them into 206—1" squares)

From assorted dark/medium prints, cut:
- ✦ 24—1⅝" strips the width of fabric, then sub-cut the strips into 564—1⅝" squares (for small version, cut 14—1" strips, then sub-cut them into 564—1" squares) **NOTE:** *Refer to the diagram on page 72 for specific color cues for the 564 hexagons—for example, the center of each Pickle Dish unit uses 4 hexagons of the same fabric, the next layer uses 12 hexagons of the same fabric, and the final layer uses 20 hexagons of the same fabric. The colors will vary according to each Pickle Dish unit because each uses a different combination of colors.*

From fabric of choice, cut:
- ✦ 2—3" x 19½" side border strips (for small version, cut 2—3" x 9¾" side border strips)
- ✦ 2—3" x 30" top and bottom border strips (for small version, cut 2—3" x 19¼" top and bottom border strips)

Design Option

This project also looks charming made in ⅜" hexagons. The finished size will be 15¼" x 17½" (not including the frame). See below for the necessary yardage and cutting instructions.

Fabric Requirements

Template

✦ ⅜ yard tan print for hexagons
✦ ⅞ yard assorted dark/medium prints for hexagons
✦ ⅓ yard fabric of choice for border

Cutting Instructions

From tan print, cut:
✦ 8 − 1⅜" strips the width of fabric, then sub-cut them into 206 − 1⅜" squares

From assorted dark/medium prints, cut:
✦ 21 − 1⅜" strips the width of fabric, then sub-cut the strips into 564 − 1⅜" squares. *NOTE: Refer to the diagram on page 72 for specific color cues for the 564 hexagons—for example, the center of each Pickle Dish unit uses 4 hexagons of the same fabric, the next layer uses 12 hexagons of the same fabric, and the final layer uses 20 hexagons of the same fabric. The colors will vary according to each Pickle Dish unit because each uses a different combination of colors.*

From fabric of choice, cut:
✦ 3 − 3" strips the width of fabric for border

Sewing Instructions

Jill used the English paper piecing method for her project.

1. Clip the corners of the squares, being careful not to trim the entire piece to ¼" from the edge of the hexagons since it is best to have a little extra fabric to work with. It is okay if the fabric overlaps a bit on the back of the hexagons. Don't worry about cutting the squares a precise size because the trimming is done only to reduce the bulk that goes to the back of the hexagons.

2. Thread your needle with a single contrasting thread and make a knot at the end. (Jill prefers to use one needle to baste and a different one to whipstitch because the template will dull the needle used to baste.) Lay the hexagon template on the wrong side of the fabric and fold over the seam allowance on one side. Stick the needle through the fabric and template from the right side of the fabric. Fold the seam allowance over to the next side, then stick the needle down from the wrong side to the right side. Fold the seam allowance over to the next side. Continue in the same manner until all sides are basted. End with a thread tail on the right side of the hexagon, which will make the paper hexagon easier to remove later.

3. Baste another piece of fabric to a template. Continue until you have enough hexagons to create the four different units shown below.

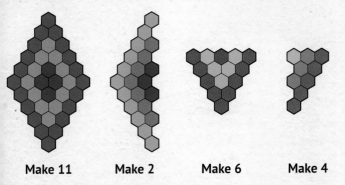

Make 11   **Make 2**   **Make 6**   **Make 4**

4. To join the hexagons, place them side by side. Using a contrasting thread (which makes your stitches easier to see), make a knot at the end. Starting at a point on the wrong side, slide your needle between the fabric and template to hide the knot in the fold through the fabric from both hexagons, being careful to catch only the fabric and not the template. Lay the two pieces flat, make a loop knot to connect both hexagons, and whipstitch along the sides you are joining. Make a loop knot at the next point. Continue adding hexagons in the same manner to create the necessary number of units noted in step 3.

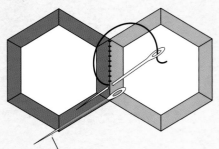

You can also slide the needle under/inside the fold to start the next piece.

5. Once a hexagon is surrounded on all sides by other hexagons, remove the basting from the one that is surrounded, then remove the template but do NOT remove the basting/template from any outer edges.

6. Referring to the quilt assembly diagram below, join the tan print hexagons and units from step 3 into diagonal rows. Note that some rows are entirely tan print hexagons and others contain both tan print hexagons and the units from step 3.

7. Using fabric sizing spray, press one side of the quilt center. Carefully remove the basting and the templates on that side only. Press again. With right sides together, sew the border strip to the quilt center, aligning their edges on the drawn lines in the following diagram. Insert a pin at each end and one in the middle. Sew the 2−3" x 19½" strips for the large version (or 2−3" x 9¾" strips for the small version) to the sides of the quilt center.

8. Sew the 2−3" x 30" border strips for the large version (or 2−3" x 19¼" strips for the small version) to the top and bottom of the quilt top in the same manner noted in step 7.

9. Wrap the borders around to the back of the frame's center board, tape them to the back, and insert the frame's center board into the frame. Jill used a second board to disguise the back for a nice, finished look.

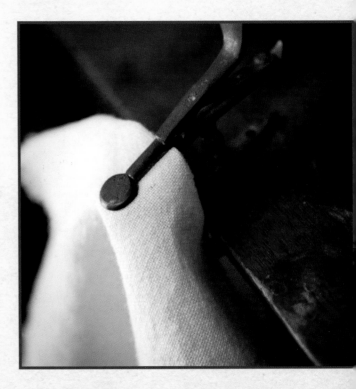

PRIMITIVE PINEAPPLE

Designed by Jill Shaulis

My fascination with small quilt pieces took on new meaning when I began foundation-piecing a Pineapple block like this one. I learned this method using 6" blocks, but wasn't satisfied until I conquered it in not only 4" blocks but nine 2" blocks as well. The strips for the latter were so small that the thickness of their seam allowances actually added a sense of depth and texture to the finished project. I enjoy displaying small projects like these in rustic frames custom-made by my brother-in-law.

Large Primitive Pineapple

Finished size: 10½" x 10½" (not including frame)   **Finished block size:** 4" x 4"

RUSTIC CHARM

Spotlight your finished projects in our weathered barn-wood frames pictured on this page and page 74. To order one, contact Yellow Creek Quilt Designs at (815) 443-2211 or yellowcreekquiltdesigns@gmail.com.

Small Primitive Pineapple

Finished size: 8" x 8" (not including frame)   **Finished block size:** 2" x 2"

Fabric Requirements

Jill made one version with four 4" blocks (pictured on page 74) and a smaller one with nine 2" blocks (pictured on this page). Yardage requirements for the smaller 2" blocks are in parentheses in the list to the right.

✦ Fat quarter light print (Fat quarter)
✦ 25–6" squares of assorted dark/medium prints (35–5" squares)
✦ 3" square dark red print for block centers (3" square)
✦ ⅛ yard black print for border (⅛ yard)

Cutting Instructions

The cutting measurements for the small version are in parentheses below.

From light print, cut:
+ 5—¾" strips from fat quarter for blocks (for small version, cut 11—⅜" strips from fat quarter)

From assorted dark/medium scraps, cut:
+ 40—¾" x 6" strips for blocks (for small version, cut 72—⅜" x 5" strips)
+ 16—1¼" x 1¾" rectangles for outer triangles of blocks (for small version, cut 36—1" x 1¾" rectangles)

From dark red print, cut:
+ 4—1" squares for block centers (for small version, cut 9—⅝" squares)

From black print, cut:
+ 2—3" x 8½" side border strips (for small version, cut 2—3" x 6½" strips)
+ 2—3" x 13½" top and bottom border strips (for small version, cut 2—3" x 11½" strips)

Sewing Instructions

1. Copy a total of four paper patterns for the large version on page 79 or a total of nine paper patterns for the small version on page 80. Instead of paper, we prefer to use a product called Fundation made especially for foundation-piecing. Cut each pattern apart just outside the dashed lines.

2. Set your sewing machine's stitch length to 1.5.

3. Place the paper, printed side down. Center a dark red print square over the #1 square center on the paper pattern. (Depending on the foundation-piecing paper product you choose, you might have to hold it up to a light source to make sure it is centered.) With right sides together, lay a light print triangle (#2) on the center square, matching the raw edges. (The light print triangle and all subsequent fabric pieces need to be trimmed so they are at least ¼" beyond the area to be covered.) If it is helpful, you can pin the pieces in place as you sew them down to the paper pattern. Turn the paper pattern over and stitch the line between #1 and #2, extending your sewing line a stitch or two beyond the intersections. Trim close to the stitched line.

4. Turn the paper pattern over and finger-press the triangle back as shown in the top diagram on page 77. Turn the paper pattern, print side down, and referring to the remaining diagrams on the next page, continue adding fabric pieces following the number order on the pattern pieces. (All numbers that point north, south, east, and west use the light print. All numbers that point to the corners use the medium/dark prints.) Be sure that the last round of strips extends beyond the dashed line of the paper pattern.

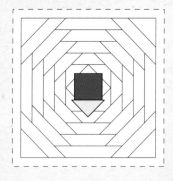

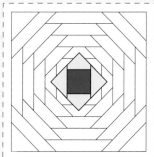

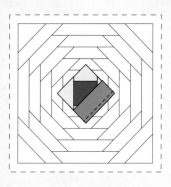

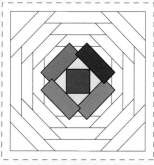

5. To hold the last strip in place when stitching blocks together later, stitch around the entire block so it falls between the last solid line and the dashed line. Trim the blocks on the dashed line of the paper patterns.

6. Sew the blocks together, using the outer solid line as your seam allowance guide. You will stitch four 4" blocks for the large version and nine 2" blocks for the smaller version. It is best to press the seams open since they are very bulky.

7. Referring to the assembly diagram below, sew the 2−3" x 8½" border strips for the large version to the sides of the quilt center. Then sew the 2−3" x 13½" border strips to the top and bottom of the quilt top.

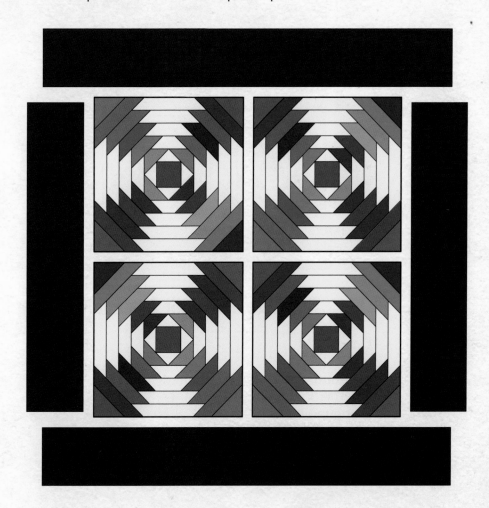

Large Version Quilt Assembly Diagram

8. Referring to the assembly diagram below, sew the 2—3" x 6½" border strips for the small version to the sides of the quilt center. Then sew the 2—3" x 11½" border strips to the top and bottom of the quilt top.

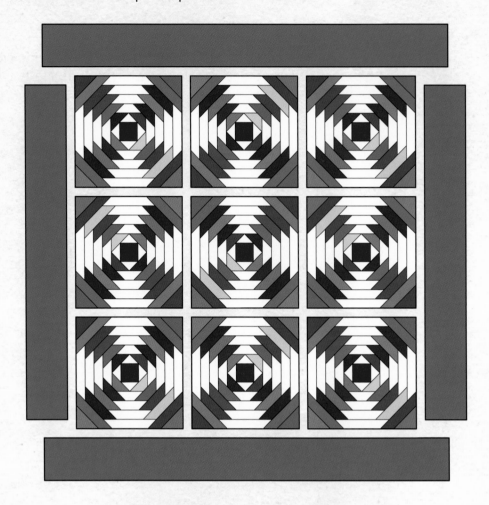

Small Version Quilt Assembly Diagram

9. Instead of quilting her quilt, Jill framed it by wrapping the border around the inner frame board and taping it to the back. To disguise the back, she placed another board on top of it.

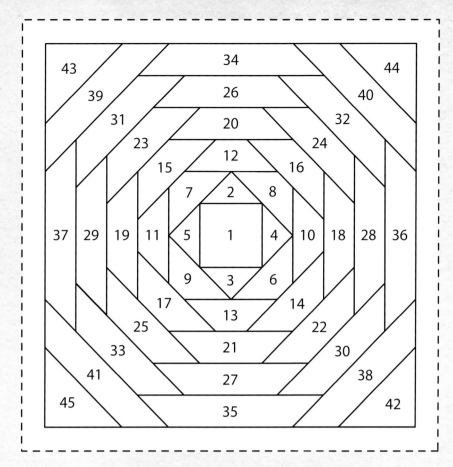

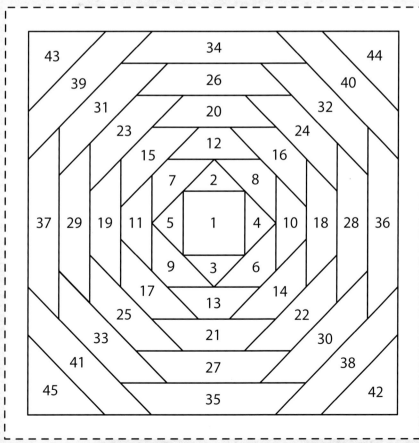

Large Version Templates

Small Version Templates